POEMS

VOLUME1

JAMES DAERRANE

Contents

Contents

1. WHAT'S IN A NAME ?

The night was bright and cold,
The moon was full and
The woman lay on her back after she
Had made love with a man whose name
She didn't know.
What is in a name, she thought,
Who is interested in a name, she thought,
The man also didn't know her name.
The man woke up and smiled against
The woman.
The man thought what a night.
He turned and looked at the woman.
You are a great woman, he said with all
The honesty of a man.
You are a hell of Woman.
The same night they make love with each other
Without knowing or asking each other names.
Indeed what's in a name.

2. THE SPANISH VIRGIN

She was just 22 years old, and she was
Still a virgin.
She had beautiful brown eyes,
and she had short nor long hair.
A Spanish virgin young and with full
Breasts that still had the same form.
She was naked in an apartment in Madrid
And she stood for a mirror.
She was waiting for the man that would become
Her lover, her husband and the man that she
Will give children.
She will become a wife and a take care of children.
The Spanish virgin in Madrid.

3. THE FEMALE BALLET DANCER.

She jumped as high as she could.
She looked with the expression of
A well trained person.
She danced with much grace and with many
Steps. How high can she jump?
The female ballet dancer.

4. THE REDLIGHT DISTRICT.

Walking in the red-light district in the
Rain. I was not motivated by anything.
The curiosity to meet women in the night.
No, I did a research on female sex workers.
However I became a client and frequently
Visitor of the redlight district.
Beautiful women you can meet in the red light
district. However their kindness is for sale and
sex is for sale.
The sex is without emotions and is purely
out of Lust. The male desire to have an ejaculation.
The enjoyment of an ejaculation.
The women only cared for the financial compensation
the money.
These experiences with these females were beneficial
For my existence.
I was in a deep hole.
And I came out
Of that hole.
The hole was deep, and it was dark.
A deep dark hole.
I came out of that deep dark hole.

5. WALKING IN THE RAIN.

I've walked in my life longer than most people
Have done. I walked in the rain. I walked in
The Snow. I slept in the rain. Almost six degrees
Below zero Celsius/21.2 Degree Fahrenheit.
I'm proud of that is the question.
No is my answer.
I'm crazy or mentally ill.
No is my answer.
I was robbed by thieves and these thieves are
Considered hardworking people. Genuine thieves.
One of these thieves has the profession as an engineer and
the other thief is a photographer.
The main female thief works as a nurse.
Beware of these thieves they are everywhere.

6. ICE, WATER, SNOW AND RAIN.

Ice.

Water.

Snow.

Rain.

Sunshine.

Man and woman.

Child.

Toddler.

Infant.

Girl.

The night.

The stars.

The moon.

The Sun.

The city lights.

The city centers.

The city queens.

The city mayors.

7. DAY AND NIGHT.

The day an event of the day
That is a beautiful event, the day
That starts with the sun uprising
The master of the world and life,
The Sun.
The light of the sun that makes
The day a beautiful event.
Making love during the day is an
Desirable event.
The night that is so dark and the
Moon that is ooh so bright against,
The night. The night the beauty of
The night.
The stars that are against the sky.
Ooh what a night it was late and it
Was ooh so bright.
Having sex in the night.

8. THEY WERE THE OPPOSITE OF EACH OTHER.

The wind blew over the island.
It was before the Sun came up.
A man a musician lay near a
Woman, a C.E.O of A Multi million
dollars company and a widow.
They were both naked and they both
Had just met each other.
They were both awake and they were
Both the opposite of each other.
They lived two weeks with each other
And they were both incredibly in love
With each other. They concluded they
Where both the opposite of each other.
At the end she left for New York.
He left for Tokyo and both went to
Their own life and they never met
each other again.

9. DAY AND NIGHT

The day an event of the day
That is beautiful event, the day
That starts with the sun uprising
The master of the world and life,
The Sun.
The light of the sun that makes
The day a beautiful event.
Making love during the day is an
Desirable event.
The night that is so dark and the
Moon that is ooh so bright against,
The night. The night the beauty of
The night.
The stars that are against the sky.
Ooh what a night it was late and it
Was ooh so bright.
Having sex in the night.

10. KATRINA KAIF.

She is a natural beauty
And an outstanding actress
An Indian beauty with a lot
Of talents.
She speaks with much grace,
She acts with much naturalism,
An Asian beauty and an out-
Standing performer.
I hope you read this poem,
I wrote it especially for you,
Without any intentions then,
A healthy urge to write.
The sun comes up and the beauty of
Morning Sun is one of the most beautiful events,
Especially if you are on the beach,
In the morning.
This comparison is the comparison I
Make when I think of Ms.Katrina Kaif,
And write this poem in the morning.
What a beautiful woman she is and an outstanding actress

11. THE FRENCH WOMAN.

The beauty of the French women.
She sat naked in the front room.
She was full of the body fluid of
A man older than her.
Did she like it and did she felt guilty.
No she liked sex and she didn't felt guilty.
The French woman in her twenties and she had
Brown hair and she had brown eyes.
She might become pregnant from this man..
She had sex without a condom, and she didn't
Used the pill.
The French women are women that are the
Most desired women in Europe.

12. I AND I AND I AND I

The vibes are felt by me the
Right vibes.
The naughty sis is a sis that is
Wet in the evening.
When I push in her I push it when my
Brains are full with ganja.
My manhood is erect as it never is.
The sis feels it especially the European
and the American sis.
These sis also like the smell of ganja and the
Vibes are hailed by them.
The smell of the burned ganja fills the
Rooms and the houses.
Because I know it's for I and I and I and I.

13. I'M A MAN.

I'm a man a middle age man.
They try to kill me from my birth on.
An unwanted child.
I'm still alive and I will live
Many years.
I'm a man I'm a man I'm a man.
I'm a man I'm a man I'm a man.
I'm a man I'm a man I'm a man.
I'm a man I'm a man I'm a man.
I'm a middle age man
A strong man and a man with
Good idea and a civilised man.
I'm a middle age man.
I'm a man I'm a man I'm a man.
I'm a man I'm a man I'm a man.
I'm a man I'm a man I'm a man.
I'm a man I'm a man I'm a man.

14. HE AND SHE

It was at night and it was raining
She ran away with tears in her eyes.
He ran behind her to come back with
To his house.
She said to him: I don't love you anymore.
I want to be far away from you.
You are not a person I want to be with.
You are a bad dream.
The both stood in the rain and he wanted
To kiss her. She turned her face to her.
She pushed him from her.
Leave me alone and don't love anymore.
What is love? he replied.
I can't love you more than I love myself.
And you can't love me more than you love
Yourself.

15. FOUR WOMEN

The morning was cold and the and the
Snow fell with any mercy.
Four women stand without any expressing
In their faces at the grave of a man they
all four loved and wanted the married with.
The preach of a religious man was heard and the
Beautiful dressed and expensive dressed women
Were not interested in the preach.
They were all from another country and the all
Travelled by train.
They were under their umbrellas, and they were
All expected to meet the sister of the man they
All four-theme loved and respected and wanted to
Married and have children with.
The morning was cold and the snow fell merciless
On the umbrellas, on the heads of the men and women
and on the grave and on the grave yard.
A religious man read a text out of the bible.

16. TWO MEN AND TWO WOMEN

Two men and two women
Were naked after they had sex
They looked at each other and the women smiled
At each other.
The men hadn't any expression in their faces.
This was in room somewhere in a city.
In another room near them was a middle age
Watching television.
It was a new program of the Island of
Aruba.
The man drank tea and watched with interest
the television program.
Near the room of the man a middle age woman
With her young lover lay naked.
The woman was a wealthy woman.
The man was in his
Begin twenties.
Three rooms in a hotel somewhere in a city
Somewhere in the northern part of Italy.

17. THE AUSTRIAN FEMALE.

In a train from Rome to Milan I met
Three females I was at time in my
Middle twenties and they were
In their begin twenties.
They were from Austria and one of them
Was the European version of the folk singer
Tanita Tikaram.
An Austrian version at that time I didn't know
Who this English female singer was.
I heard the song Twist my Sobriety and I seen
The artist on the television once or twice.
The calmness and the way she spoke was immense
And it was the first time I met a woman with some-
Much intensity.
This Austrian female told me her of her desires
And about her wishes. Her idea of life.
I was impressed and we liked each other for the
moment we were on the train.
In Milan I departed the train and
I never saw her again.
She travelled further to Wien Austria.
I wonder what became of her. I believe she is in her

Country a successful woman.

18. MEN ARE GOOD.

Men are good and men have
Created a world that is labelled.
As a high-tech world with a legislation
And men is capable to control all of the
World meaning earth.
Men must be proud of that.
Men will achieve more and men
Must not be sabotage in his effort
To organize the world.
There are groups of people that want
to Sabotage Men in its effort.
And this all for a big laugh.
And for the sake of being funny.
They portrait men as mindless murders,
Child abusers and all other unlawful
Practices.
Some of these people are the richest men
In the world.
Men are good and men must be proud of that.

19. TOTAL TOUCH.

Trijntje Oosterhuis what must I say
About this remarkable singer and woman.
A lot in terms of her profession.
Unfornately I'm not personally acquitted with
This female singer.
I was informed while I lived in the Netherlands
That her brother had telephoned me.
However if that was a joke or not I don't
Know.
Trijntje & Tjeerd Oosterhuis the main member of
The former popgroup Total Touch.
Personally I liked their music and they are both still
Outstanding artists and performers.

20. BEAUTY EXISTS

Beauty exists and it is
Around. Everywhere and don't
Neglect it.
Your beautiful wife
Your beautiful Son
Your Beautiful daughter
Your beautiful house
Your beautiful car.
If you look around you and
Observe and look at what
Is around you will see and
Appreciate beauty.
The beautiful sun
The beautiful moon
The beautiful sea
The beautiful art painting
First most find yourself beautiful.

21. THE FRENCH WOMAN IN PARIS.

She was naked and she looked
At the man that was beside her.
He was asleep and he had a satisfied
Expression in her face.
Somewhere in a luxurious modern apartment
In Paris.
She didn't know the name of this man.
She never asked him his name.
What is important in a name?
The sun was just coming up and she
Was fully awake.
Did she felt any guilt?
No, she didn't do any illegal thing.
A French woman in her begin twenties in
Paris after she had sex with a man she
Didn't the name of.
She stood up and her attractive appearance
Was visible against the upcoming of the sun.
A French woman in Paris.

22. LIFE.

Darkness
Sunrise
The morning nakedness
The evening beauty
A man
A woman
A child
The happy family
The good educated man
The caring full woman
The sunny island
In the Caribbean
The good man
The good woman
The proud father
The proud mother.

23. HE WAS HELPLESS.

It was raining and she ran,
Away from the man she didn't love
Anymore.
The man ran behind her and stopped her.
She said I don't love you anymore.
They both stood in the rain.
In the cold rain.
At night.
I love you he said.
More than anything.
I don't love you anymore she said crying.
You are not the man I want to be with.
You will not change.
You will be the same.
You will not change.
You don't love me anymore.
You love yourself and all the
Others you need somebody else.
I'm not that person.
She ran away from him.
He stood and looked at her and
he was helpless.

24. SLEEPING WITH THE ENEMY

One night I was at a man
His home. I spoke over the
Possibility to be involve in
A cinematographic work and
Over the investment that will
Be involved in this film project.
After I left I went to a film work
With the name sleeping with the
enemy.
I personally don't believe that
the man is the enemy of the woman.
However in this film work you could
Say.
That man was not a man that I
Personally liked.
The film work itself was a well produced
Film work.

25. S.C.U.M.

This means Society to Cut Up Men
Open.
My fellow men and women be aware of these
People.
They are dangerous people and are a society
Of men haters.
Men need women such as women need men.
Men best friends are women.
Together we form a society and together we have
Built this planet.

26. WHY DID YOU LEAVE?

The naked body of yours I
Miss in the morning.
I don't hear you singing anymore.
I'm a lost man without you.
Why did you leave still puzzles me?
Why did you leave?
Why didn't you say to me that you
Weren't happy?
The smell of your body I still smell.
The movement of your body I still see.
I miss that all.
I still love you more than anything.
I especially miss your naked body.
Your voice and the songs you sing
Every morning.
Why did you leave?
Why did you leave still puzzles me?
Why did you leave?
Why didn't you say to me that you
Weren't happy?
The smell of your body I still smell.

27. DECEIVERS

There are people that want to deceive us and are specialized in
deceiving us.
Important people. Rich people. Are among
Them.
Their assistants in this act deceiving
Are often common people. Not rich people.
They will often try to influence somebody in
Your family or a close friend of yours.
To participate in their acts of deceiving.
Be aware of these deceivers.
They will steal everything you own and they
Will misuse you family or your close friends.
Important people. Rich people. Are among
Them.
Be aware of these deceivers.

28. FADING GIGOLO

I enjoyed watching this movie.
Typical a product of a New York
Based filmmaker.
The Jazz music is also typical
For these kind of film works.
Especially the actress Sofía Vergara,
is performing well and her character
is impressive.
The whole film work is a well produced
and well acted film work.
Fading gigolo, a man that receives a
Financial compensation for sexual encounters
With females.
Eventually two of his main clients want to
Perform a ménage a trois.
That remains me of the song just a gigolo
Everywhere I go.
Fading Gigolo.

29. MUTUAL BENEFIT.

How are you today?
I'm feeling well I have
Nothing to complain off.
Was the answer.
The world is not perfect.
If you want to complain you
Have the right to.
People are becoming further by using
Other their skills or their financial
Means.
Some of them want to use you
And some of them want to get used
By you.
That is how the world and life is.
To envy to progress in life is a
Good virtue. Do it civilize.
I also believed in mutual interest
And into that both parties involve
Must benefits positively of any
Collaboration.

30. THE MALE BALLET DANCER

The strength of the male ballet
Dancer is known in the world.
Strong man and a man with
The vision to dance.
The male ballet dancer.
He dances as he has never dance before
The strength and the male strength is
Know for years, centuries.
A man is a strong individual.
Stronger than a woman.
In the dance of the male ballet dancer
The strength is shown.
A strong man.
The male ballet dancer.

www.ingramcontent.com/pod-product-compliance
Lightning Source LLC
Chambersburg PA
CBHW021153130726
47988CB00004B/1591